C000047227

Tiger Salamanders

Biology, Husbandry and Breeding

Jens Benthien

Copyright: © 2018 Jens Benthien
Editing: Erik Kinting / www.buchlektorat.net
Cover & layout: Erik Kinting
Photos: © Jens Benthien
Translation: www.herprint.com

Published & printed by: tredition GmbH, Hamburg, Germany

This publication, including all its parts, is copyrighted. Its exploitation is prohibited without prior written authorization by the publishers and the author. This applies in particular to its multiplication by electronic or other means, translation, distribution, and making it available to the public.

Bibliographic information of the German National Library:
The German National Library („Deutsche Nationalbibliothek") has recorded this publication in the German National Bibliography; detailed bibliographic data can be obtained online from http://dnb.d-nb.de.

CONTENTS

INTRODUCTION

This book is dedicated to the captive care and propagation of North American Tiger Salamanders. It is intended to raise the interest in these impressive and long-lived animals on the one, and surely contains the one or other useful pointer or idea for those terrarium keepers who have already gained insights into the keeping of Tiger Salamanders on the other hand.

Tiger Salamanders are well suited to the beginner in keeping amphibians if he or she will adhere to certain fundamental husbandry directives. Irrespective of this, the representatives of this species complex are attractive to the more experienced keeper of amphibians as well, since propagating them in captivity is not without a few challenges.

Tiger Salamanders have been known as terrarium animals since the beginning of the last century. In the past, they used to be collected in large numbers and on a commercial scale from the wild, which made them low-priced animals that were readily available in the pet trade almost all the time. This situation did certainly not promote the interest in these species in general and even less encouraged attempts to propagate them in earnest in particular. Such "consumption" of large numbers of wild-caught animals resulting from a lack of knowledge of their biological needs and disinterest in producing them in captivity was, and is, not acceptable, however.

Following a brief foray into the systematics, distribution and ecology of these salamanders in nature, the focus of this book is on describing in detail how to house, feed and propagate them in human care. Moreover, a few lines of his book are each dedicated to discussing the ability of these animals to become sexually mature while remaining at larval stage (neoteny), the problem of hybridizing, and the possible appearance of color mutations.

A male of the Eastern Tiger Salamander (A. tigrinum) on his way to a spawning pond after hibernation

TAXONOMY

Tiger Salamanders form part of a genus commonly known as Mole Salamanders, or in scientific taxonomy, the genus *Ambystoma* TSCHUDI, 1838, which presently consolidates about 33 species. The so-called *Ambystoma tigrinum* complex makes up the greatest group both genetically and morphologically within this genus and occupies the widest distribution range of all ambystomatids.

The scientific generic name makes reference to the bluntly pointed snout of these animals, which is particularly clear from the alternative spelling "*Amblystoma*" that is often found in old literature. It is composed of the Greek words *amblys* = blunt and *stoma* = mouth. For its part, the name *Ambystoma*, which is the valid name today, is thought to be based on a misspelling in the original description by TSCHUDI (1838).

The English vernacular name commonly applied to *A. tigrinum* and *T. mavortium*, "Tiger Salamanders", obviously refers to the dorsal color pattern of these two representatives of their genus, whereas the alternatively used denomination "Mole Salamanders" is directly adopted from the generic vernacular name and makes reference to the secretive and often subterraneous ecology of these animals. One German name for them, "Querzahnmolch" (="across-toothed salamander)", is interesting insofar as it refers to their palatine teeth being arranged in cross rows.

The cladistic relationships between the species in the family of Mole Salamanders are fairly close so that hybridization with fertile offspring in both sexes are no phenomenon exclusive to captive setups, but also occur in the wild.

The famous Axolotl, *Ambystoma mexicanum* (SHAW, 1789), which has all but been extirpated in its native Mexico, is likewise quite closely related to other Mole Salamanders.

Axolotl (Amblystoma tigrinum). ⅔ natürl. Größe.

"This illustration of a metamorphosed axolotl illustrates the confusion riddling the naming of the genus in the 19th century. (Brehms Tierleben, Volume 7, Bibliographisches Institut Leipzig und Wien, 1892)"

TAXONOMIC STATUS

The taxonomic history of Mole Salamanders is one of continuous changes that have been continuing right to the present. In the past, the North American Tiger Salamander was classified as a species with six subspecies, and it was only when variation in the mitochondrial DNA (SHAFFER & MCKNIGHT 1996) and morphological differences (IRSCHICK & SHAFFER 1997) were discovered that the eastern form, *Ambystoma tigrinum* (GREEN, 1825), was granted the rank of a species in its own right in the more recent past.

In accordance with their geographical distribution, three genetic evolutionary lines could be identified in *Ambystoma tigrinum*: a northeastern group (in the northeast of the Great Plains), a southeastern group in the central parts of the United States, and a West Florida group.

The remaining five subspecies were reallocated to the Western Tiger Salamander, *Ambystoma mavortium* BAIRD, 1850, whereas the Californian Tiger Salamander, *Ambystoma californiense* GRAY, 1853, and the Mexican Tiger Salamander, *Ambystoma* velasci DUGÈS, 1888, were each recognized as separate species.

Left: A. tigrinum from Florida, center: A. tigrinum from Georgia,
right: A. tigrinum from Illinois - all are adults

SYSTEMATICS (RAFFAËLLI 2013)

Class:	Amphibia
Subclass:	Lissamphibia
Order:	Tailed amphibians – *Caudata*
Superfamily:	Salamanders – *Salamandroidea*
Family:	Mole Salamanders - *Ambystomatidae*
Genus:	True Mole Salamanders – *Ambystoma*
Species:	*Ambystoma tigrinum* Ambystoma *californiense* *Ambystoma velasci* Ambystoma *mavortium*
Subspecies:	*Ambystoma mavortium mavortium* *Ambystoma mavortium stebbinsi* *Ambystoma mavortium utahense* *Ambystoma mavortium diaboli* *Ambystoma mavortium melanostictum* *Ambystoma mavirtium nebulosum*

DISTRIBUTION

The distribution range of Tiger Salamanders extends from southern Canada through wide parts of the US from the east to the west coast and south to central Mexico. With its various subspecies, *Ambystoma mavortium* inhabits the largest portion of this area. A precondition for their occurrence is access to suitable breeding waters, for which reason their range is patchy in places. Tiger Salamanders are believed to be absent from the Rocky Mountains, New England, and the Appalachians.

Eastern Tiger Salamander, *Ambystoma tigrinum* GREEN, 1825

Ambystoma tigrinum – adult male

The Eastern Tiger Salamander sports a yellowish to olive spotted dorsal pattern on a brown to black ground color. The sizes of these spots vary significantly with the origins of specimens. Those from the southern parts of the range furthermore appear to grow to smaller adult sizes than their cousins in the north. The range of this taxon extends from New York state south down the east coast to Florida and west as far as Nebraska, Kansas and eastern Texas.

Barred Tiger Salamander, *Ambystoma mavortium mavortium* BAIRD, 1850

The Barred Tiger Salamander is marked by a vertical, beige to yellow barred dorsal pattern on a dark brown to black background, with the "barring" varying with the individual population. Its distribution range stretches from Nebraska to the southern parts of Texas and west to central Colorado and New Mexico.

Ambystoma mavortium mavortium – adult female

Arizona Tiger Salamander, *Ambystoma mavortium nebulosum* HALLOWELL, 1853

Arizona Tiger Salamanders (see Fig. page 21) are dark brown to blackish with yellow spots or reticulations on their backs. The resulting pattern is usually finer and less dense than in the nominate form. Salamanders of this taxon are encountered in central Colorado and New Mexico west to Utah and Arizona.

Spotted Tiger Salamander, *Ambystoma mavortium melanostictum* BAIRD, 1860

This form of the Tiger Salamander typically sports a branching pattern of thin, dark markings that will often be connected and so form a network of lines. The ground color is light olive to gray. Its distribution range extends from the southern and southwestern parts of Alberta and Saskatchewan in Canada south to northwestern Colorado and Nebraska. Isolated populations are said to exist in western Washington state and eastern Idaho.

Ambystoma mavortium melanostictum – adult female

Gray Tiger Salamander, *Ambystoma mavortium diaboli* DUNN, 1940

The ground color of these Tiger Salamanders ranges from a dark shade of olive green to yellowish brown and carries a pattern of scattered, fine spots on the back and flanks. They are native to Canada (Saskatchewan and Manitoba), northwestern Montana, North Dakota, South Dakota, and the extreme west of Minnesota. The subspecific epithet makes reference to its occurrence in the area around the "Devil's Lake" in North Dakota.

Ambystoma mavortium diaboli – adult male

Sonora Tiger Salamander, *Ambystoma mavortium stebbinsi* **LOWE, 1945**

The Sonora Tiger Salamander is highly variable as far as its color pattern is concerned, with individuals usually resembling those of the subspecies *nebulosum* or *melanostictum*. It is found in the Huachuca and Patagonia Mountains of southeastern Arizona.

Californian Tiger Salamander, *Ambystoma californiense* **Gray, 1850**

The Californian Tiger Salamander is native to the central and western lowlands of California. This species exhibits yellowish to cream-colored, round or oval spots on a grayish black ground color that may sometimes have a bluish sheen.

Ambystoma californiense – adult female

Mexican Tiger Salamander, *Ambystoma velasci* DUGÈS, 1888

This Tiger Salamander is distributed at higher elevations in northern Mexico. Its color pattern consists of a dark brown to black background with scattered, yellow or olive green spots on the back and flanks.

The Mexican Tiger Salamander (A. velasci), here semiadult specimens (Photo: Manuel Gonzalez)

The Mexican Tiger Salamander (A. velasci) also occurs in a neotenic form in its natural habitat. (Photo: Manuel Gonzalez)

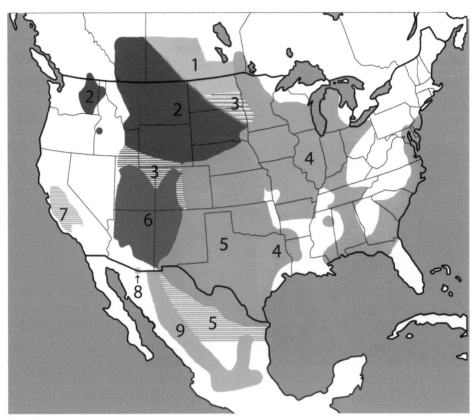

Simplified representation – Map not to scale

1. Ambystoma mavortium diaboli
2. Ambystoma mavortium melanostictum
3. Overlapping distribution ranges
4. Ambystoma tigrinum
5. Ambystoma mavortium mavortium
6. Ambystoma mavortium nebulosum
7. Ambystoma californiense
8. Ambystoma mavortium stebbinsi
9. Ambystoma velasci

The problem of identification

It is not always a straightforward affair to tell Tiger Salamanders apart from one another and identify their subspecific affinities, because the color pattern of one and the same taxon may vary widely from one region to the next. This may even be the case within the same population, and the facts that some distribution ranges overlap and these salamanders can produce fertile hybrids certainly do not make this task any easier.

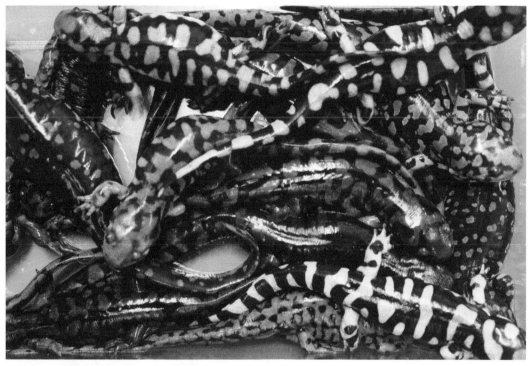

Variability in the color pattern of the Tiger Salamander

A. mavortium ssp.

Ambystoma mavortium nebulosum (Foto: Stefan Greff)

An aggravating factor in this conjunction is that Tiger Salamander larvae are very popular as fishing bait in the US and widely traded under the name "water-dogs". Demand for them is fuelled by a multitude of contributions in literature on hobby fishing that describe in glowing terms triumphant catches of predatory fish by using these larvae on fishing hooks. To this end, the larvae are collected on a large scale and marketed in many parts of the country. Escaped or discarded bait specimens then have the potential of polluting the aboriginal fauna and mixing with locally native populations.

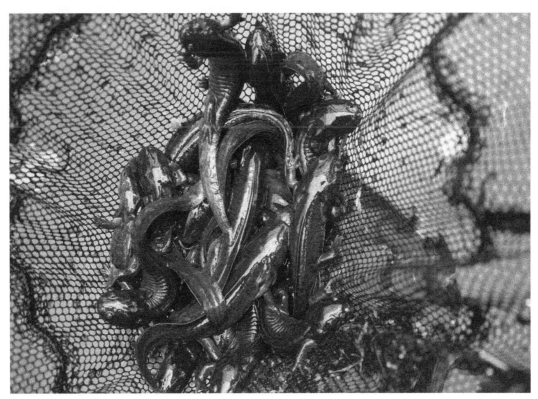

Larval Tiger Salamanders are popular as live bait for predatory fish among sports fishermen in the US.

Consequences of the nationwide displacement of larval Tiger Salamanders

Aside from rendering it difficult to identify local subspecies, this praxis of polluting local faunae may have much more dire consequences, though. Studies have demonstrated that larvae in the fishing bait trade are often infected with pathogens such as *Ranavirus* and chytrid fungus (*Batrachochytrium dendrobatidis*) that flourish under paltry storing conditions and are then dispersed nationwide. Most seriously affected by this praxis is the Californian Tiger Salamander, which now does not only have to compete for resources with *Ambystoma m. mavortium* introduced thus, but also has its genetic makeup watered down by hybrids resulting from the cross-mating of these two taxa. Owing to the so-called heterosis effect, these hybrids display greater vitality and growth rates ("hybrid vigor") than either of the parent taxa and are therefore able to drive the aboriginal Californian Tiger Salamanders from many parts of their original distribution range. As a result, *Ambystoma californiense* has meanwhile been categorized as "Endangered" as per the criteria of the International Union for the Conservation of Nature (IUCN).

Ethological differences

Aside from the studies mentioned above that have led to the taxonomic separation of the species *Ambystoma tigrinum* and *mavortium*, keeping these salamanders in a terrarium will also reveal subtle differences in their behavioral expressions. Most obvious in this regard is that *Ambystoma tigrinum* is much more secretive than *Ambystoma mavortium*. While *Ambystoma mavortium* will present itself very agile when handled and try to escape on the surface or climb out of its terrarium, *Ambystoma tigrinum* will rather respond by attempting to bury itself in the ground like a mole. Even though these two species are equally proficient ground workers, *Ambystoma mavortium* will bury itself in the soil so that it is completely submerged in the substrate whereas *Ambystoma tigrinum* will establish tunnels with compacted walls if the type of substrate permits it. Such a tunnel will often end in a small chamber that is large enough for the salamander to turn around. Being an ambush hunter, *Ambystoma tigrinum* usually sits in the exit of its shelter waiting for prey to come within striking range. Any perceived threat will then see it disappear into the depths of its tunnel with surprising speed.

In contrast to these two species, *Ambystoma californiense* is hardly ever seen digging in the soil in a terrarium and will rather make use of existing cavities in the ground, which corresponds to its ethology in the wild.

NATURAL HABITAT

Life in the wild

Tiger Salamanders are extremely adaptive, with their individual forms being distributed from the arid fringes of deserts through forests and marshes, pastures and steppes to Alpine regions at elevations of up to 3350 m (PETRANKA 1998).

Outside of their mating season, they have a crepuscular to nocturnal, exclusively terrestrial lifestyle. They will bury themselves in damp soil, find shelter under dead wood, or re-use the burrows established by other animals. As for *Ambystoma californiense* in its rather arid grassland habitats, these burrows are most often used for retreating.

Persisting periods of drought are dealt with by the salamanders simply by staying put in sufficiently damp shelters. They have not been described as observing periods of strict estivation (summer dormancy), though.

Tiger Salamanders are still quite frequently seen in many parts of North America, but even they experience increasing pressures from the destruction of their natural habitats today. Factors affecting them very badly are not only the draining and overbuilding of these, but also include, for example, the introduction of predatory fish to their breeding waters.

Within the food chain, even fully grown Tiger Salamanders serve as prey to a wide range of predators. Their options for defending themselves are rather limited. In fact they can only try to flee and/or rely on a massive excretion of slime from their skin when facing a predator. This slime will then envelop the entire salamander in a milky and very sticky coating that renders it both unpalatable to the attacker and difficult to secure. More rarely will these animals assume a defensive stance by coiling up the body, lowering the head, and lifting the tail distinctly over the level of the dorsum (see Fig.); sometimes slow snaking motions of the tail tip may be observed in addition. In a terrarium, this response may occasionally be triggered by suddenly exposing the salamanders to bright light in the course of maintenance work inside their enclosure, for example. Altogether, the arsenal of defensive measures available to them will certainly be quite unfit for effectively deterring predators in many instances. The resultant losses among Tiger Salamanders are compensated by a correspondingly high reproduction rate.

REPRODUCTION IN NATURE

The breeding season of these salamanders is correlated to the climatic conditions in their local natural habitats and extends, with few exceptions, from March through well into summer. Mating activity is triggered not only by rising temperatures, but usually also by heavy rains and corresponding drops in barometric pressure. Precipitation will then temporary water bodies in certain

places that are suitable for breeding. Permanent, small, fish-free ponds, water-filled ditches, and waterholes for livestock are also utilized for spawning.

Being "explosive spawners", the salamanders migrate simultaneously to their spawning sites in their numbers, with the males often arriving there a few days before the females. Oviposition then takes place shortly after mating by every female attaching several hundreds to more than a thousand eggs to rough-surfaced underwater structures such as branches.

A close-up shot of oviposition – a female Tiger Salamander presses her cloaca against a submerged twig that she holds in place with her hind legs while attaching her eggs.

The initially very large numbers of hatchling larvae quite rapidly decrease over the period they need to grow and develop into terrestrial salamanders (metamorphosis). Aside from falling victim to predators, the often very prominent tendency towards cannibalism among the larvae also plays an important role here.

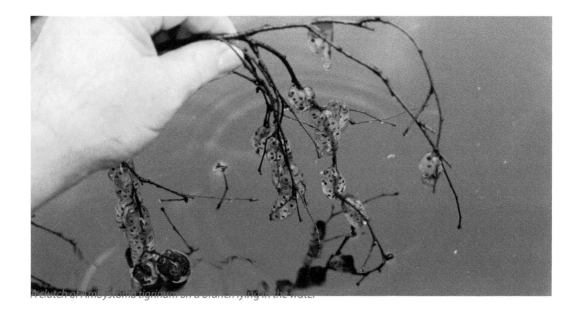
A clutch of Ambystoma tigrinum on a branch lying in the water

Cannibalism

In the case of falling water levels and the resultant shortage of food and space, a few larvae will become dominant over their siblings in a phenomenon known as the crowding effect. Apparently induced predominantly by tactile stimuli between the larvae in their shrinking habitat (HOFFMANN & PFENNIG 1999), some specimens will grow a flatter, wider head with a correspondingly larger set of teeth that also contains an additional row of teeth. Equipped thus they are now able to predate upon other larvae, even if these are only minimally smaller than they. The result of this cannibalistic intake of potent protein will be that these larvae grow at enormous rates. At a first glance, this phenomenon of turning against representatives of their own species may seem to make little sense, but closer examination will soon reveal that it is actually only a very consequent survival strategy in that not even diminishing resources can prevent at least a small number of individuals to develop into land-going salamanders that can ensure the survival of their species.

Cannibalistic and normally developed larvae of Eastern Tiger Salamanders (A. tigrinum) compared

MORPHOLOGY

Appearance

Tiger Salamanders rank amongst the largest terrestrial salamanders. In some populations of the western species *Ambystoma mavortium*, individuals regularly grow to total lengths in excess of 30 centimeters, and lengths of as much as more than 40 cm have been recorded on occasion. *Ambystoma californiense* is the smallest representative of this group, reaching total lengths of only about 20 cm.

Tiger Salamanders have a large, depressed head with a bluntly tipped snout and distinctly protruding eyes. The body is elongate and muscular with 11 to 14 costal (rib) grooves. The limbs are equally muscular, with the hind feet ending in five toes and the front feet carrying only four toes.

Representatives of the subspecies A. mavortium diaboli rank among the largest and most muscular individuals of the entire genus.

The skin

Consisting of varyingly sized spots and squiggles, the dorsal markings of Tiger Salamanders vary significantly with the population, with colors ranging from olive green through beige to brown and black. The markings are always clearly set off from the ground color, though.

The skin serves as a sensor for environmental cues such as contact, pressure and temperature. With Tiger Salamanders never drinking, but rather absorbing moisture from their surroundings via the skin, the latter is also key to controlling both the body temperature and levels of body fluids. The skin furthermore acts as a breathing organ through which oxygen is taken in to a certain degree both underwater and on land. To fulfill all these functions, the naked skin has to be kept moist because it is sensitive to desiccation.

As a protection measure against outside influences, the skin of Tiger Salamanders is equipped with glands that produce a mildly toxic substance and can be excreted in an active manner in surprisingly large amounts in situations where the animal feels threatened (see above). Its primary function is, however, to keep the skin moist at all times and provide protection against fungal and bacterial pathogens.

Because Tiger Salamanders grow throughout life whereas their skin does not, they need to molt at intervals in order to replace the old skin that has become too tight with a new, more fitting layer. With juveniles growing much faster than adults, they will molt at correspondingly shorter intervals.

As can be noted when raising larvae in a captive setting, the coloration of the skin is influenced by both the intensity of light and the shade of color of the bottom substrate. Kept on dark soil and at a low lighting level causes them to develop a comparatively darker pigmentation than when they are kept in lighter surroundings. This phenomenon must surely be regarded as an adaptation to their environment in nature and the avoidance of detection by predators.

Life expectancy

Information on the life expectancy of Tiger Salamanders varies substantially, but an age of 25 years has been reliably documented from captivity (MUTSCHMANN 2010). While these animals can be kept at room temperature all year round, it may be safe to presume that cooler temperatures in winter that enforce a period spent hibernating and the associated temporary reduction of their metabolism have a beneficial effect on their lifespan.

Various field studies investigated the average life expectancy in the wild and revealed, unsurprisingly, that some individuals lived longer than others, but the average lifespan in nature will certainly be significantly shorter than in captivity where about all of the natural threats are eliminated.

Tiger Salamanders rarely display defensive behavior to this extreme extent

HUSBANDRY AND PROPAGATION IN HUMAN CARE

Acquisition

Tiger Salamanders are regularly available from pet shops. Often, these animals are wild-caught specimens whose exact point of origin is unknown. Purchasing these wild-caughts may be problematic in that it will by no means be safe to suppose that they are not weakened from transport or even carriers of disease. Their immune system may also have been compromised from stress factors such as high temperatures, mechanical damage, water deficiency, inadequate food supply, and crowding. All these factors will then be conducive to a mass proliferation of pathogens that would not normally affect the health status of the animals and cause diseases to become acute.

It is therefore a positive development that pet shops these days also often stock captive-bred specimens. Considering that captive breeding requires some input of time and money, these specimens cannot possibly be priced as low as wild-caught ones, however. Acquiring captive-bred salamanders is nevertheless worth the extra expense, because it will minimize the risks detailed above, help conserve wild populations, and support captive breeding initiatives.

Another place where to purchase specimens is at a one of the many reptile fairs that are organized at intervals. They often offer opportunities of talking to breeders who might be able to provide information on where exactly the breeder animals originated. There are also various market places on the Internet where animals are offered for sale and breeders can be contacted directly for insider information and advice.

Quarantine

Newly acquired specimens should always be housed in quarantine initially. This means they should be accommodated under particularly hygienic conditions in a place away from the established collection. Strict quarantine is a most effective tool to prevent the introduction of diseases if it is continued for an adequate period of time. New animals may be carriers of a wide range of pathogens without exhibiting any symptoms of disease. Quarantine offers the opportunity to detect these, evaluate the general appearance and behavior of the new arrivals, and assess their food intake as well as their droppings. Diagnostic procedures and, if necessary, medical treatments can be carried out under the guidance of a veterinarian without risk to other animals.

Containers suitable for quarantine accommodation are made from glass or plastic, can be kept clean and disinfected with ease, and allow for observing in detail the metabolism and molting of the animals. The bottom should be covered with moist cellulose that needs to be replaced at regular and frequent intervals. Droppings obtained thus should be checked for obvious signs of parasites and sent to a pathology lab for analysis if in doubt. A simple artificial shelter should not be missing, though. All tools (like, e.g., feeding tweezers) and things that have come in contact with the quarantined animals or their enclosures must be disinfected right after use and not be used in other terraria, too. Wearing suitable one-way gloves when working in a quarantine tank is a good practice to prevent the spread of germs to the existing collection; otherwise washing hands with a disinfectant afterwards is a must. They will also protect you from possibly harmful pathogens even though chances of becoming infected with an animal disease (zoonosis) are very slim.

Housing

Tiger Salamanders are large and massive for which reason they will require adequately spacious terraria from about 80 x 40 cm in floor space for two specimens. Terraria with ventilation surfaces on two opposing sides are ideal, but a large air-permeable cover may also work. Because these animals are not territorial, keeping colonies irrespective of sexes and sex ratios is entirely possible. The terrarium may be made from glass or plastic, with the latter being a feasible and cost-effective alternative if larger numbers of salamanders are to be accommodated. Keeping them in enclosures out of doors is also possible at temperate latitudes as long as these are set up in a shaded spot. Such enclosure must of course be outfitted in the same manner as an indoor terrarium (see below). An outdoor enclosure needs to be made particularly escape- and intruder-proof all around on the sides and have an equally secure cover. In this respect, all locally occurring natural predators from shrews to herons and their capabilities must be taken into consideration. If the salamanders are to spend the winter in such an enclosure as well, it must furthermore be reliably secured against sub-zero temperatures.

Setting up a terrarium

As has been mentioned in the introduction, Tiger Salamanders spend a lot of their time digging in the ground. This need should be accommodated by providing a bottom substrate that is at least 20 cm deep and rests on top of a drainage layer of coarse gravel or expanded clay. Suitable as substrate are forest soil or a mix of forest soil and peat without any additives. Natural forest soil contains a host of very useful microorganisms, for example bacteria that convert the harmful ammoniac arising from the conversion of the salamanders' droppings, or springtails (Collembola) that will feed on the molt fungi thriving in the damp ambience of a salamander terrarium.

Coir, the coconut fiber substrate widely used in terrarium keeping, cannot be recommend for use in a damp terrarium, because it tends to grow moldy quickly under these conditions. A product that grows on palm trees cannot be expected to be a substitute for forest soil with its wealth of microorganisms, even if it may look similar.

The substrate should not be too finely structured, as this would make it difficult for the salamanders to bury themselves and favor excessive compacting of the soil. It should also be kept only moderately moist, because if it were too wet, the salamanders would again be unable to dig in it, not to speak of the increased risks associated with compromised hygiene. When the salamanders are active on the surface, they like to make use of shelters in the shape of clay or cork tubes. Other constituents of the decoration may include natural moss, leaf litter, tree bark, pieces of roots and rocks.

The terrarium may also be outfitted with live plants, with one suitable example being the robust Devil's Ivy (*Epipremnum*). This plant can cope with relatively little light and tolerates both temperature and moisture level fluctuations. Live plants should be left in small pots in order to protect their roots from damage through the earthworks of the actual inhabitants.

If rocks are used, attention must be paid to their not becoming a hazard to the salamanders when they dig under them. In general it must be clear that an elaborate decoration may satisfy the esthetic desires of the terrarium keeper, but will surely require more maintenance work and render it more difficult to monitor and ensure the necessary hygienic standards than in the case of a minimalistic setup that will just serve its purpose.[1]

The terrarium should be positioned in a cool to moderately warm spot, which will strike a sun-exposed place from the list of options right from the start. The target temperature here is a maximum of 23 °C. *Ambystoma*tids from temperate climatic zones are said to be active within a range from 1 through 26.7 °C (comp. MUTSCHMANN 2010). Experience has shown that they can survive temporary exposure to values as high as 30 °C without suffering adverse effects, but they should not be made to face stress factors like these unnecessarily. Not everything the animals can tolerate for a short while will be beneficial to them. On the other hand, Tiger Salamanders become active already at temperatures of just a few degrees above freezing point so that their terrarium can do without heating. Artificial lighting will likewise be unnecessary if the terrarium receives some daylight. If this proves inadequate, a source of light may be installed to create the required day/night and annual rhythms and provide the live plants with the light they need to survive.

---

1 When setting up a terrarium, clear distinctions must be made between what serves the esthetic perception of the keeper and what satisfies the biological needs of the terrarium inhabitants. Both requirements may be justified, but the needs of the terrarium animals must always come first.

A simplistic, purpose-oriented terrarium for keeping Tiger Salamanders

Access to water

Even though Tiger Salamanders can do without access to open water for a long time if only the soil is damp enough, they should nevertheless find a water-filled container in their terrarium. This container should be large enough for them to submerge themselves fully in it and to turn around. As they will often enter the water for molting, it is a good idea to place a rough-surfaced rock in it at which they can peel off the old skin. Although salamanders never drink, they will use a temporary stay in water for rehydrating via the skin. This option will become even more crucial if the terrestrial section of their terrarium should actually be too dry. The water in this reservoir must of course be replaced at regular intervals, especially as the animals will often defecate in it.

A Tiger Salamander (A. m. mavortium) in its water bowl

Terraria for Tiger Salamanders are often outfitted with very large aquatic sections, with keepers thinking that this would make the artificial habitat even more authentic. If you take a closer look at how Tiger Salamanders live in the wild, however, you will soon realize that you can just as well save yourself the trouble of installing a water-filled section in their terrarium. In nature, these animals will actually take to water only very occasionally outside of their breeding season. In day-to-day operations, fixed aquatic sections will instead require frequent cleaning and are notorious for springing nerve-racking leaks. That Tiger Salamanders cruising through a terrarium that contains a large aquatic section will find and end up in the latter earlier or later is beyond question, as is the fact that their keeper will then be able to observe them nicely. Such luxury is not a necessity, though.

FEEDING

Suitable foods

Tiger Salamanders can be fed with live prey such as various species of crickets, roaches, waxworms, grasshoppers and moths. The nutritional content of crickets can be substantially improved by first keeping and feeding them for a while with high-quality feeds, as well as dusting them with a suitable mineral powder right before offering them to their final consumers. Although practiced by many keepers, the use of earthworms as the basis of their feeding regime must be viewed critically as it bears a risk of overfeeding. Tiger Salamanders are actually quite clumsy when it comes to predating upon earthworms if they are not assisted by making the worms available from tweezers. This curious lack of skill is explained by the fact that earthworms have been absent from the North American habitats of Tiger Salamanders at least since the last Ice Age[2]. They exhibit much more refined skills if their prey comes walking along on a few legs.

The diet can be complemented by occasional offerings of strips of turkey or chicken heart, baby mice, or freshwater fish. Even though more dated literature contains recommendations of feeding salamanders with the meat of warm-blooded animals, this food should actually be limited to exceptional treats while the diet should be a widely varied as possible.

---

2 It was not before the arrival of the European settlers that various species of earthworms returned to the United States, and by now, these are considered harmful neozoans. The fishing bait marketed under the name "Alabama Jumper" (Amynthas agrestis), for example, is a species originating from Asia, while the European lobworm (Lumbricus terrestris) that has likewise been introduced to the US and is used as fishing bait and feeder animal is known there as the "Canadian Night Crawler". The invasive earthworms from Europe and later also from Asia today cause havoc in the terrestrial ecosystems of North American deciduous forests in that they accelerate the composting of the protective layer of leaf litter that is essential to the survival of various plant and animal species depending on this particular stratum.

Feeding and feeding behavior

If the salamanders are fed mainly with live food, their terrarium should not be oversized in order to ensure that they will encounter their intended prey sooner rather than later and to avoid that perished feeder animals become a health hazard. Tiger Salamanders will often lay in wait right beneath the soil surface for prey to come by and try and grab the insect when it comes within range. Hungry specimens will leave their shelters and actively approach potential prey, though. If a prey item is faced with the front of the snout, it will be attacked in some kind of "snap leap" in which the salamander jerks forward towards the prey item while trying to grasp it at the same time. If the approach is more from the side, the snapping motion will be combined with a quick, lateral contortion of the body, which secures the prey item in most instances.

Tiger Salamanders quickly become used to fixed feeding times and taking food from tweezers. While this type of feeding surely requires more effort from the keeper it has the advantage of ensuring that every specimen can be monitored as to its food intake and persistent non-feeders can be identified beyond doubt and in time. In the latter scenario, a certain degree of tolerance must be advised, because these animals just have the habit of disappearing underground and not feeding for a week or two every now and then and without a reason being apparent.

Tiger Salamanders will quickly learn to take food from tweezers and often rush towards the keeper when he approaches their terrarium.

Captured prey is swallowed whole. If a prey item is particularly large or has been secured across the mouth it will first be positioned properly for ingestion; if it fights back, it will first be dazed by shaking it violently.

Predation also takes place underwater, with the salamanders apparently using their senses of taste and/or smell for detection. Prey is located by scouring the bottom while swinging the head from side to side and snapping at objects that could potentially be prey the moment they are touched with the snout.

Adult Tiger Salamanders do well when fed once or twice every week, but juveniles should receive food every day, simply because the frequency and volume of feeding determine their growth during this phase.

HEALTH ISSUES

This section has deliberately not been titled "Diseases" since it is meant to focus once more on the aspects that will ensure that the salamanders stay healthy in the first place.

As has been mentioned before, Tiger Salamanders are very robust animals and not at all prone to contracting diseases. The chapters dealing with acquisition, husbandry and feeding have already described what their keeper needs to do to prevent health problems from surfacing..

Pathogens often turn into a problem only when their host animals are neglected in their captive setting. Bacteria and fungi, for example, are organisms that are commonly present in small numbers on the animals themselves or in their immediate environment all the time without causing them any harm and no need for the keeper to worry about them. They only become a threat when they are allowed to accumulate in an unhygienic environment and/or proliferate on or inside weakened animals so that they become the source of an opportunistic infection.

If symptoms surface despite all care and discipline at one stage or another, the keeper will soon find himself at his limits if he does not happen to be a veterinarian specialist, especially as a large number of diseases may have very similar symptoms. Examples of this category include a range of alterations to the skin such as patchy or spotty, darkening discolorations, but also lumps and open, festering wounds. Emaciation may point to an underlying health problem just as much as a sudden increase in girth due to water retention. Other warning signs include, for example, hyperactivity alongside being on the surface all the time, lethargy, and long-term disinterest in food. Changes in the normal locomotion, like partial paralysis, uncoordinated movements, and cramp-like contortion of the body, must likewise be taken seriously.

By now, there are, fortunately, a number of veterinarians who specialize in treating reptiles and amphibians. But even these specialists will not come up with a diagnosis without assessing the afflicted animal and taking adequate diagnostic measures such as the microscopic examination of swabs and fecal samples. If an apparently diseased animal has died, it might make sense to send it to a veterinarian pathology lab for establishing the exact cause of death. These results plus expert advice from your vet may in the end save the rest of your collection.

HIBERNATION

A period of winter dormancy (hibernation) is not really a must to keep Tiger Salamanders healthy. It is only when it comes to breeding with specimens originating from the more northern parts of their distribution range that temporarily keeping them in a cool situation will become a precondition, because they form their sexual products during this period. The assumption that failing breeding attempts may be a result on breeder specimens originating from areas with greatly different climatic conditions is a widespread one, but it is also entirely possible that this aspect is greatly overrated. Successful propagation depends on a variety of factors and may not be reproducible every year even if the approach remains about the same. Considering that the salamanders have to somehow handle non-standardized conditions in the wild as well, synchronization of the intended breeder specimens appears to be much more important.

Before entering their winter dormancy, the salamanders should be in a state of good health and well fed. They are transferred to their hibernation containers when temperatures are constantly low, but around mid-December at the latest. Overwintering them is possible by a variety of means and can be effected in a refrigerator, at adequate cool latitudes also in a basement shaft, or even in an unheated greenhouse, hotbed or similar structure out of doors.

Overwintering outdoors

If the salamanders are kept out of doors at temperate latitudes, the natural cooling of the weather can be made use of. Overwintering them outside requires of course that the animals themselves are protected from a direct impact of frost. This is achieved by making available a substrate that is deep enough for them to bury themselves to beyond the danger zone where they will be safe from freezing to death. Selecting a protected spot for their containers in the first place therefore makes sense. If particularly frosty weather persists, the construction may need to be additionally secured with sheets of polystyrene, for example. As far as monitoring the conditions is concerned, a thermometer with a temperature probe that will reach down to the deeper layers of the substrate might be a good investment.

The salamanders' winter quarters can be made from a wide range of materials as long as they are safe both from the salamanders escaping and predators, rodents in particular, entering. They need to be furnished with covers that will facilitate an adequate exchange of gases and a certain influx of natural light, but also protect the container from precipitation that could turn the substrate into mud. On the other hand, there must be a certain degree of substrate moisture, and for this reason it will be necessary to check it at regular intervals. The substrate should feel damp and be crumbly when a handful is picked up, but it should not clump. With moisture evaporating all the time, it may feel too dry after a while and must then be remoistened by spraying it with water. I use a mix of forest soil and pure peat, as these two constituents store water well. Covering the substrate with a layer of leaf litter or moss is a good idea, because this provides additional insulation. Some specimens will respond to warmer phases during their hibernation period by temporarily moving up into this top layer. It is not uncommon for some individuals to become awake and a little active and there is nothing the keeper will have to do or worry about if this happens. Experience shows that they will return to deeper layers earlier or later and continue to hibernate.

Feeding is unnecessary during hibernation and would surely be very difficult to effect anyway. This means that the salamanders should be transferred to their winter containers only when outside temperatures permit you to do so, i.e., when they are constantly low at near freezing point during the nights and not higher than 10 °C during the days. This will ensure that the animals reduce their activity levels and not use up important energy reserves that they will need during their period of dormancy. If they were kept in a terrarium inside the house before, temperatures must be reduced gradually in preparation.

When this type of overwintering is applied, it will often suffice to just take the cover off, let natural precipitation dampen the substrate, and make the salamanders wake up once spring has started returning.

Tiger Salamanders can be overwintered in hotbed-like structures out of doors.

Overwintering in a basement shaft

The general pointers given for overwintering salamanders out of doors of course also apply for letting them hibernate in a basement shaft or an unheated outbuilding. These locations lend themselves to this purpose, because they offer low winter temperatures, yet carry a much smaller risk of the hibernation containers freezing through. The only difference actually is that the keeper has to have a closer eye on their moisture content in spring and emulate the spring rains manually, or transfer them to an outside spot at the right time.

Polystyrene containers are well suited to overwintering Tiger Salamanders in a basement shaft, for example.

Overwintering in a refrigerator

Salamanders can be overwintered in ordinary plastic terraria in a refrigerator. These containers surely offer the best opportunities for monitoring the animals and this method has no alternative in warmer regions. With the inside temperature set at about 4-6 °C, the animals need not bury themselves deeply, which would also be difficult given the limited space inside a fridge. Moisture levels must be checked in this scenario as well, of course. Because the animals are isolated from outside weather conditions, the keeper will have to decide when it is time to let them terminate their winter dormancy. At temperate latitudes,

cues to this effect can be derived from keeping an eye on the activity of indigenous amphibians: once the native toads start migrating in their numbers, it may also be time for the Tiger Salamanders to wake up and focus on reproduction.

A refrigerator for overwintering facilitates perfect control of temperature and humidity while virtually locking out all other environmental influences..

PROPAGATION AND RAISING JUVENILES

Matching breeder specimens

Important preconditions for successful reproduction will include that the intended breeder specimens are in good health and old enough. Breeding attempts often fail because the animals that are used are too young or have not been properly conditioned both as to their level of fat reserves and/or synchronized by a preceding hibernation period. If the point of origin of your breeder specimens is known, you should by all means try and conserve this local form and not cross it with any others. Even if you, with the best intent, match specimens that are phenotypically similar but of unknown origin, you may be in for some major surprises with regard to the colors and patterns in the resultant offspring.

Mating phenotypically similar specimens of uncertain origins will often produce unexpected offspring (parental specimens left and right)

Breeder specimens should be at least two, better three years of age. Observations in human care have shown that *Ambystoma californiense* will become sexually mature not before reaching an age of four or five years. Sexing is fairly easy on the basis of secondary sexual traits during the reproductive season, which is when the cloacal glands of the males will swell and the tail may grow a higher fin; otherwise their tails are longer, and they are also slimmer overall. Females ready to mate lack the swollen cloacal region, but exhibit a slight elevation instead, which will also distinguish them from females not ready to mate.

Ambystoma californiense grows a particularly conspicuous tail fin during the mating season.

Particularly rotund females may carry eggs, but this is not necessarily an indicator for their being conceptive. These exterior morphological traits diminish to varying extents outside of the breeding season, so that sexing might be a little more difficult then.

Cloaca of a male Tiger Salamander – A. tigrinum

Cloaca of a female Tiger Salamander – A. tigrinum

Conditioning

As has been outlined above, the moisture content of the soil in the overwintering container needs to be raised in early spring (March/April). An exception is *Ambystoma californiense* whose mating season will begin already in December. This species may benefit from an artificial raining system of the kind used for propagating various anurans for emulating the heavy winter rains it would experience in its natural range. If the salamanders were overwintered out of doors, they may well be left right in their hibernation quarters and exposed to the first natural rains. My observations indicate that they will respond to this by appearing on the surface quite promptly. They can then be collected and transferred to a spawning tank for mating. The latter should offer a water level of some 40 cm and can be likewise placed out of doors where it will be exposed to natural sunlight and rain. Solar radiation, as well as natural rain hitting the water surface, are often considered stimuli for mating, but at least will not do any harm. The spawning tank should be outfitted with some twigs or similar objects that reach to the water surface and so enable the salamanders to rest there without any effort on their own. Round or oval containers are preferable over rectangular ones because they will not stop the animals in their forward motion in a corner when they follow each other in courtship. As for the water temperature, this detail should also emulate the conditions in the wild and therefore be only a few degrees Celsius above freezing; if the container is placed outside, this factor will take care of itself by default. A spawning container should be simplistic and serve only its intended purpose, yet large enough for the salamanders to move about quite freely. It may be outfitted with a perforated brick, for example, whose holes will serve to anchor some twigs of willow and birch. These twigs will then be readily accessible to the salamanders for spawning and can be removed and transferred to other containers with ease. A few beech or oak leaves as well as some aquatic plants may be added to provide cover and help stabilize the water quality. Aquatic plants are used for spawning only if there are no better alternatives for doing so.

A breeding tank set up outdoors, ready to receive the selected breeder specimens

Mating

As has been mentioned before, the males will usually arrive at the spawning site a few days before the females. This aspect should be respected by placing the females in the intended spawning tank only several days after the males. If the salamanders are ready mate, you will soon, at the latest after dark, see them engaging in courtship activities. Initiated by pheromones released by the female, a pair will circle each other, and the male will push the female over the bottom of their water body, trying to position himself under her and, so to say, levering her off.

Ambystoma californiense courting

The male will also lift his tail and use it to fan water towards the female. If the female is interested in his advances, she will eventually follow him and pick up with her cloaca one of the often numerous spermatophores that he has by now deposited on the bottom and so facilitate the process of internal fertilization. A spermatophore consists of a gelatinous, cone-shaped foot that carries a whitish packet of sperm on its tip.

If the intended breeder specimens exhibit disinterest in letting themselves sink to the bottom and frantically try to escape from the tank right from the start instead, you may safely suppose that they are not interested in mating and you should abort the attempt on the following day at the latest.

A spermatophore

If they accept the container, but display no courtship activities even after several days, you may want to try and motivate them by reducing the water temperature by means of exchanging the water or adding some ice. Matching different partners might sometimes also do the trick. If, however, no mating activities ensue even then, the trial should be aborted after a fortnight at the latest and the animals returned to their terrestrial terrarium. Experience has shown that waiting any further makes no sense in this situation: there will simply be no reproduction during this season, and an enforced stay in the water will only exhaust the salamanders. No matter how much care and effort you may have invested into preparing your specimens, there is never a guaranty for success, and nobody will be able to tell you why an attempt failed. Sometimes these salamanders simply insert a year in which they will not reproduce.

Oviposition

Eggs are deposited from about 24-72 hours after mating and females may continue to lay eggs for several days. While *A. mavortium* and *A. californiense* will deposit their eggs individually or in strings like the Axolotl, *A. tigrinum* attaches its eggs in small clusters on the branchwork in its spawning tank.

A Tiger Salamander busy laying eggs (Ambystoma californiense)

A Tiger Salamander busy laying eggs (Ambystoma m. mavortium)

For raising the resultant larvae, the adult specimens have to be removed from the tank or, better, the twigs must be removed from it and transferred to other containers for their further development now. Otherwise there is a risk of the adults consuming the eggs. They may also excessively pollute the water and so cause the eggs to grow moldy.

The eggs should be recovered pretty promptly from the tanks holding the adult specimens and transferred to, e.g., plastic buckets to ensure their development in a controlled environment.

If the eggs are fertile, their nuclei will start losing their spherical shape after a few days. The subsequent developmental stages of the eggs can be followed very nicely by means of a magnifying glass. Hatching of the larvae is heralded by brief bursts of hectic movement inside their eggshells.

Depending on the water temperature, the larvae will hatch after about two to four weeks. However, if the eggs are left in a container outside and exposed to very low temperatures, no development may be discernible to the human observer for weeks on end before the environmental conditions have eventually improved.

Eggs at various stages of development. Left: Ambystoma m. mavortium, right: Ambystoma tigrinum.

A larva of A. m. melanostictum shortly before hatching

Housing the larvae

If you wish to raise a larger number of larvae, you will need to have a larger number of suitable raising containers at your disposal.

A simple method of housing larvae in plastic containers

Small larvae can be housed in plastic buckets for the first few weeks after hatching, and in larger, stackable plastic containers thereafter. They should be sorted by size at regular intervals during the course of raising them. Together with feeding them generously, this measure will prevent larger larvae from attacking smaller siblings or even transform into the cannibalistic morph that has been described above.

If you wish to raise Tiger Salamander larvae in large numbers you will need to sort them by size at regular intervals in order to prevent cannibalistic larvae from forming.

The larvae of *Ambystoma tigrinum* are particularly aggressively disposed towards each other, whereas the larval offspring of *Ambystoma mavortium* will typically be much more compatible.

The larvae may of course be kept one by one as well. This approach will surely require more effort and space, but evade the described problems and ensure that every individual can develop in optimal conditions. A high water quality must be ensured throughout the raising process, for which reason the water may need to be replaced on a daily basis. Smaller colonies of larvae may otherwise also be raised in aquaria equipped with filter systems. An aquarium offers a perfect opportunity to watch the development and intraspecific behavior of the larvae. Its water level should be gradually lowered when the larvae start exhibiting signs of intending to go onto land soon.

A larva of A. mavortium diaboli

Larval development

Right after hatching from their eggs, the larvae will typically lie motionless on the bottom of their raising tank. It is only after two to three days, and after they have resorbed their yolk sacs, that they will become active and start feeding. Suitable starter food exists in the shape of live *Artemia* nauplii or small *Daphnia*.

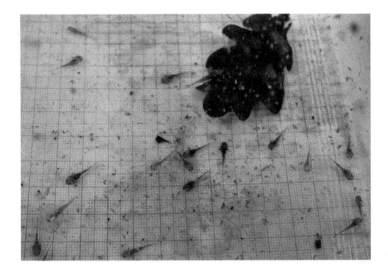

Young Tiger Salamander larvae are easily fed with Daphnia and other pond plankton. Shown here are one week-old larvae of A. m. mavortium.

That they indeed take in food is visible to the observer by their performing small "leaps" when they snap at prey. These are the result of their sucking in the tiny organisms by opening the mouth in a flash. The resultant negative pressure draws the prey into the mouth and the larva forward at the same time. This method of ingesting food is also known as "hyoid pumping" and maintained right to metamorphosis.

After two to three weeks into raising, the larvae will have grown enough to now also be able to handle live mosquito larvae, *Tubifex* and enchytraeans. The front legs will have appeared by this point of time, but the development of the hind legs takes much longer.

A while later, your supplying them with live prey will become unnecessary, with the larvae now readily feeding on defrosted frozen mosquito larvae. As they grow, their menu can be widened to now also include shredded fish meat, poultry heart, small earthworms, and similar types of food.

Feeder pellets of the kind also used for raising Axolotls may likewise be accepted, even if these may not be particularly popular in the beginning. Group-raised larvae need to be monitored quite closely then, because they might decide that their siblings are much more to their taste.

The characteristic flattened head of a larval A. m. diaboli with the three gill branches on either side of the head

From the praxis of the author's it appears that the larvae of *Ambystoma mavortium* can be adjusted to accepting these pellets from a size of about 5 cm quite easily, but various experiments to this effect failed altogether in larval *Ambystoma tigrinum*.

In order to prevent larvae from going for and injuring each other, an exchange of their water must always be followed by offering them food right thereafter. Otherwise, confused by the suddenly changed water chemistry, they will commonly mistake their siblings for prey and losses must be expected. Once a larva has been injured thus, it can only be saved if it is separated from its siblings on the spot. Larvae detect food, amongst others, with their well-developed olfactory sense, and excretions from an open wound will make them identify an injured sibling as prey.

Injured larvae will therefore be relentlessly attacked and eventually killed. However, when raising larvae in colonies, incidents like these cannot always be prevented by the keeper, and if a larva is rescued in time and raised in isolation, it tends to recover quickly and impress its caregiver with its enormous regeneration capabilities that equal those known from the related Axolotl.

Progressing metamorphosis and associated changes in the color pattern of Ambystoma mavortium

Sensory performance of larval Tiger Salamanders

Like many other aquatic amphibians, larval Tiger Salamanders are equipped with pressure and electro-receptors, which enable them to locate moving prey (HERRMANN 1994). Changes in the pressure within the water caused by prey

animals moving are registered via the lateral line organ that extends from the head down the lengths of the flanks.

The depressions of the lateral line organ in the skin surface are well visible in this larval Tiger Salamander.

For its part, the ampullar organ serves the localization of prey by being sensitive to changes in the electric field that result from muscle contractions of moving prey animals. These pressure and electro-receptors will in the same manner also signal an approaching predator and trigger escape behavior.

The salamander larvae are furthermore furnished with a well-developed olfactory sense (of smell or taste) whose receptors are located on the surface of the tongue and the floor of the oral cavity. These receptors enable them to also identify and locate unmoving food. Their sense of vision, on the other hand, is rather poorly developed and likely to be of secondary importance in the dark and in murky water.

Larval Tiger Salamanders appear to orient themselves relative to their surroundings by means of their "parietal eye", also known as the pineal organ or "third eye". This is an evolutionary very old, light-sensitive organ situated in the center of the parietal bone in the skull that is pointed straight up and used for detecting differences in light intensity, distinguishing between top and bottom.

Scientific studies have demonstrated that neotenic Tiger Salamanders apparently base their entire spatial orientation on information obtained via the pineal organ, apparently employing some kind of compass that is kept trained on the direction of incoming solar radiation all the time (TAYLOR & ADLER 1978).

Metamorphosis

Metamorphosis refers to the switch from an aquatic to a land-living animal that is typical for a mphibians and will turn larvae that breathe via their gills and skin into terrestrial salamanders that breathe with lungs.

The larvae of Tiger Salamanders metamorphose into terrestrial animals after three to four months, depending on factors such as food availability, temperatures and population density. Some individuals will metamorphose even only in their second year of life from larvae that have grown to substantial sizes. The water temperature for raising larvae should range between 16 and 22 °C, with lower values slowing their development down.

A juvenile A. californiense whose color pattern is as yet incompletely formede

That metamorphosis is due soon is heralded by the eyes of the larvae becoming more projecting, the fins continually reducing in height, and the gill branches shrinking. Also, the skin of the larvae will become firmer now and start showing the first indications of the eventual color pattern, even though it will usually be a few more months before juveniles exhibit it in full.

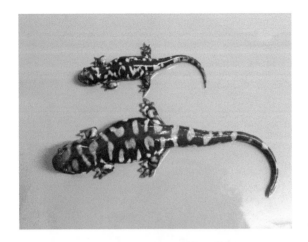

Ambystoma m. mavortium,
juvenile and adult

Ambystoma m. melanostictum,
juvenile and adult

Ambystoma tigrinum,
juvenile and adult

When you start noting that the time of metamorphosis has arrived, the water level in the nursery tank should be reduced to just a few centimeters so that the salamanders will be able to reach the water surface without effort.

Larval Tiger Salamanders come to rely more and more on breathing via their lungs during the course of their metamorphosis.

They now depend more on their lungs for breathing, and there is a distinct risk of them overexerting themselves or even drowning in deep water. Making available some easily scaled rocks or simply placing their tank at an angle will provide them with options for exiting the water.

Placing the nursery tank at an angle will allow metamorphs to go onto land easily.

Once you find them largely outside the water, it will be time to collect and transfer them to a terrestrial terrarium outfitted with damp moss. Here, they will fairly soon start predating upon adequately small insects such as crickets.

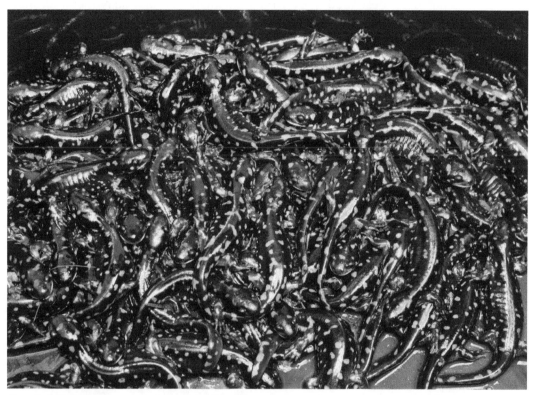

Juvenile A. tigrinum, the result of a successful breeding season

NEOTENY

As has been described above, Tiger Salamanders habitually metamorphose and develop from their aquatic larval form into terrestrial salamanders that will return to their spawning waters only for the purpose of reproduction. Some western populations are, however, noteworthy for their increased tendency towards neoteny. This term describes individuals that become sexually mature in their larval form. Neotenic specimens are fast-growing, become sexually mature earlier, and are capable of producing more eggs per clutch than their land-living cousins, which all can have advantages for the survival of the species in certain situations. In water bodies bare of fish, neotenic Tiger Salamanders rank amongst the top predators and serve as an effective control mechanism that will keep the populations of competing species and predators in the shape of predatory insects in check. Despite their status, these animals are able to mate with the terrestrial cousins of their species, producing offspring that may metamorphose or remain neotenic as well (facultative neoteny).

Tiger Salamander larvae can reach impressive sizes if they remain at this stage for more than a year.

Neoteny is more commonly observed in populations that are faced with periods of excessive drought at least seasonally and offers the affected species an option for survival. If, for example, the terrestrial population is largely wiped out by climatic extremes, the neotenic population, whose larvae are able to metamorphose at least in part, will be able to repopulate the surrounding land once more when circumstances have eventually improved. If unfavorable climatic conditions persist, on the other hand, a repeated collapse of the land-living population may cause a genetic manifestation of neoteny, the loss of the ability to metamorphose, and leave this population tied permanently to its breeding waters. The Axolotl, *Ambystoma mexicanum*, which can usually be made to metamorphose through the artificial application of thyroid hormones (inducible-obligatory neoteny), provides the most widely known example for this scenario (WISTUBA 2011).

"Wild-colored" terrestrial form of the Axolotl (A. mexicanum)

Some species, including the famous olm (*Proteus anguinus*), have even become insensitive to externally provided thyroid hormones and will remain in their aquatic form no matter what (obligatory neoteny).

77

COLOR MUTATIONS

Spontaneous alterations to the color pattern are occasionally found amongst the larvae even of entirely normally colored parent salamanders. These anomalies are usually genetically induced and may affect both the ground color and the pattern. There may be a partial loss of color intensity (hypomelanism) or even a complete lightening of all colors (albinism), but also an overall darkening (melanism) of the taxon-specific coloration.

A Tiger Salamander (A. tigrinum) with reduced pigmentationng

These anomalies occur both in the wild and in human care. Conspicuously colored specimens hardly stand a chance of establishing themselves in nature, however, as they are more readily detected by predators. It may furthermore be presumed that these specimens are less readily accepted by a mating partner. Even if they were, color anomalies are usually inherited recessively and would therefore make no appearance in the offspring from such an abnormally colored specimen and a normally colored one; the anomaly would simply be lost in subsequent generations within the entire population. This scenario is a little different in captivity. Here, recessively inherited traits may be more common due to related specimens being mated.

Quite a range of color varieties have been bred and combined in this manner in the closely related Axolotl, *Ambystoma mexicanum* – interestingly, all albinistic Axolotls are based upon one albinistic Tiger Salamander collected from the wild (see below).

Unusually colored captive-bred animals will of course attract the particular interest of a breeder, and one tends to treat these specimens with particular care. In praxis, however, it has turned out that these color deviations are not rarely linked to various other genetically induced anomalies, and many of these conspicuous larvae will typically perish before completing their development. Specimens noteworthy thus often exhibit slowed growth compared to their siblings, are more susceptible to health problems, and possess only reduced regeneration capabilities. Various expressions of malformation of the locomotor apparatus and irregular metamorphosis may be observed as well.

Various color morphs of the Axolotl (A. mexicanum)

Color mutations

Leucistic and albinistic terrestrial Axolotls (A. mexicanum)

A Tiger Salamander larva with lightened colors next to a normally colored sibling

A Tiger Salamander larva with lightened colors

HYBRIDIZING

As has been mentioned before, a close cladistic relationship exists between Tiger Salamanders and the Mexican Axolotl (*Ambystoma mexicanum*). It is therefore not surprising that these two taxa have been crossbred on many occasions, for example by the geneticist Rufus R. HUMPHREY (1892-1977), who published in the 1960' (1967) on the successful experiment of crossbreeding an albinistic Eastern Tiger Salamander female collected from the wild in Minnesota with a male Axolotl. All "gold albinos" of the Axolotl today are based on this one crossbreeding experiment in which HUMPHREY artificially inseminated the eggs of the albinistic Tiger Salamander female with the sperm of a leucistic Axolotl in his laboratory.

Successful experiments involving the same species had previously also been conducted and described in Germany in the 1940' (GEYER & FREYTAG 1949). The hybrids arising from such cross-breeding are robust animals with a high growth rate and a fairly wide variety of color patterns. Almost all of them will later metamorphose, and the same will be true if these hybrids are again cross-mated among each other. The young of this second generation will then be more divergent, tending to the one or the other grandparent species, and identifying these as what they really are is notoriously difficult.

Studying the cross-breeding of species is surely a thrilling topic and may produce interesting results, but also something that just cannot be encouraged in terrarium keeper circles. From a perspective of species conservation, keeping captive breeding colonies of Tiger Salamanders pure must definitely be given preference. Looking at the subject objectively, cross-breeding has by now been documented well in word and pictures, quite exhausting the potential of new revelations. In fact, continued cross-breeding poses a risk of compromising the acceptability of keeping amphibians in terraria and the credibility of captive breeding in the public eye. Moreover, there is a risk in this conjunction that the continued impact of Tiger Salamander hybrids on Axolotl bloodlines will further contaminate the gene pool of the latter species, causing its tendency to metamorphose to increase. Even now, many keepers are today flustered to a certain extent by the pet trade offering animals under various inventive trade names that can only be presumed to be crosses for a number of years.

Hybrids A. mavortium x A. mexicanum of the second generation (Photo: Ralph Kopp)

Left: A. tigrinum, center: Hybrid A. tigrinum x A. mexicanum, right: A. mexicanum (Photo: Hanna König)

Left: A. mavortium, center: Hybrid A. mavortium x A. mexicanum, right:. A. mexicanum (Photo: Hanna König)

OTHER SPECIES OF THE GENUS *AMBYSTOMA*

Aside from Tiger Salamanders, a range of other representatives of the genus *Ambystoma* can be encountered in the terraria of enthusiasts, including, for example, *Ambystoma gracile*, *Ambystoma macrodactylum*, *Ambystoma opacum*, *Ambystoma laterale*, and *Ambystoma maculatum*. These must also find mention here, especially as some of them are propagated with quite some success in captivity as well.

Ambystoma talpoideum

Ambystoma gracile

Ambystoma macrodactylum

Ambystoma opacum

Ambystoma laterale

Ambystoma maculatum

The husbandry requirements of the mentioned terrestrial species are not all that different from those described above for Tiger Salamanders. While they may sport rather interesting color patterns, they will usually grow to smaller adult sizes, and their ecologies are typically even more secretive than those of Tiger Salamanders. They are actually rarely seen outside their shelters during daylight hours, and opportunities for observing their habits will be limited to the time after dark.

Some of these species have developed very interesting reproductive strategies indeed, and these are described here in brief.

The Marbled Salamander, *Ambystoma opacum* (GRAVENHORST, 1807), has managed to become largely independent from water as far as courtship, mating and oviposition are concerned. The female will deposit her eggs in a damp depression in the ground in the immediate surroundings of a body of water and guard them until the winter rains arrive and flood the depression and the eggs. The larvae will then develop in the water, but never return to it once they have metamorphosed (BLANCK 2007).

Blue-spotted Salamanders, *Ambystoma laterale* HALLOWELL, 1856, typically share their natural habitats with other species of *Ambystoma* (*Ambystoma texanum, jeffersonianum*, and *tigrinum*) and commonly interbreed with these. Another particular is that some parts of their distribution range host all-female populations. These females carry triploid sets of chromosomes and will use the sperm of the males of other species of *Ambystoma* merely for stimulating oviposition, but without making use of their genetic information (chromosomes). This rare phenomenon is known as gynogenesis (AVISE 2008).

Spotted Salamanders, *Ambystoma maculatum* (SHAW, 1802) for their part will enter into a stunning type of symbiosis with green algae. The latter will infiltrate the embryos during their development inside their eggshells, apparently benefiting from their nitrogen-rich metabolic products whereas the embryonic salamanders take advantage of the oxygen produced by the algae in the conversion process of these. It is presumed that the algae are passed on from one salamander generation to the next at least in part. Symbioses of this kind, i.e., in which plant and animal cells cooperate directly, had not been known from a vertebrate prior to this discovery (KERNEY et al. 2011).

Next to the Axolotl that has already been mentioned, two other neotenic species from Mexico are kept in aquaria, i.e., Anderson's Salamander (*Ambystoma andersoni* KREBS & BRANDON, 1984) and Duméril's Salamander (*Ambystoma dumerilii* [Dugès, 1870]). Like the Axolotl, these species of *Ambystoma* are seriously threatened in their continued existence in the wild, if not already at the brink of extinction, as a result of human activities. It is therefore fortunate that some dedicated keepers have been very successful in propagating them in captivity.

Ambystoma andersoni

Ambystoma dumerilii

Ambystoma mexicanum

ACKNOWLEDGMENT

This is the place where I can say Thank-you to all the persons who have contributed in a major way to the evolution of this book.

I am particularly indebted to Dr. Uwe GERLACH for critically reviewing my manuscript from an expert perspective and his helpful comments. I thank Steffen HELLNER for sharing with me information on the keeping of salamanders, their habits in the wild, and for making available to me many of my breeder specimens. Ralph KOPP is thanked for his numerous suggestions and for letting me use some key illustrations. I thank Markus WEGMANN, Lars HARTWIG, and my daughter Annika for their helpful input and suggestions during the penning process of my manuscript, and my son Max for his support in caring for and raising the animals portrayed in this book. Daniel LISCHKE is thanked for helping with the realization of the graphic used in this book. Manuel GONZALEZ, STEFAN GREFF, and Hanna KÖNIG are thanked for making their photographs available.

I thank Erik KINTING for his competent tutorship during the realization process of this book project, and Sabine ABELS for giving it its attractive layout. I owe a great Thank-you to Thomas ULBER (www.herprint.com) for his excellent translation of my book into English.

REFERENCES:

Geyer, H., Freytag, G. E. (1949): Über Kreuzungen zwischen Tigersalamander (*Ambystoma tigrinum*) und Axolotl (*Ambystoma mexicanum*) und ihre F2 Generation – Rat der Stadt Magdeburg / Kulturamt, S. 9 - 23

Hoffman, E. A., Pfennig, D. W. (1999): Proximate cause of cannibalistic polyphenism in larval tiger salamanders. – Ecology 80(3): 1076 - 1080

Mutschmann, F. (2010): Erkrankungen der Amphibien – Enke Verlag, 334 S.

Petranka, J. W. (1998): Salamanders of the United States and Canada – Smithsonian Institution Press, Washington, 592 S.

Raffaelli, J. (2013): Les Urodeles du Monde, 2. Auflage – Penclen Edition, Frankreich

Wistuba, J. (2008): Axolotl, 2. Auflage – Natur und Tier Verlag GmbH, 93 S.

Shaffer, H.B., M. L. McKnight (1996): The polytypic species revisited: genetic differentiation and molecular phylogenetics of the tiger salamander (*Ambystoma tigrinum*) (Amphibia: Caudata) complex. Evolution, 50:417-433.
The Polytypic Species Revisited: Morphological Differentiation among Tiger SalamanderTigesalamanders (*Ambystoma tigrinum*) (Amphibia: Caudata) Author(s): Duncan J. Irschick and H. Bradley Shaffer Source: Herpetologica, Vol. 53, No. 1 (Mar., 1997), pp. 30-49

Bogart, J.P., Licht, L. E. (1986): »Reproduction and the origins of polyploids in hybrid salamanders of the genus *Ambystoma*«. Canadian Journal of Genetics and Cytology 28 (4): 605–617.

Avise, John (2008): »Reproduction in the semichaste: Gynogenesis, hybridogenesis and kleptogenesis«. Clonality: The Genetics, Ecology, and Evolution of Sexual Abstinence in Vertebrate Animals. Oxford: Oxford University Press.

Taylor, H., Kraig Adler: The pineal body: Site of extraocular perception of celestial cues for orientation in the tiger salamander (*Ambystoma tigrinum*) Journal of comparative physiology December 1978, Volume 124, Issue 4, pp 357-361

Kerney, R., Eunsoo, K., Hangarter, R. P., Heiss, A. A., Bishop, C. D., Hall, B. K. (2011): Intracellular invasion of green algae in a salamander host. Proceedings of the National Academy of Sciences of the United States of America (PNAS) 108: 6497-6502

Riley, S. P. D., Shaffer, H. B., Voss, S. R., Fitzpatrick, B. M. (2003): Hybridisation between a rare, native tiger salamander (*Ambystoma californiense*) and its introduced congener. Ecological Applications 13:1263–1275

Herrmann, Dr. H. J. (1994): Amphibien im Aquarium – Ulmer Verlag, 167 S.

Herrmann, Dr. H. – J. (2001): Terrarienatlas Band 1 – Mergus Verlag, 1152 S.
Blanck, T. (2007): Querzahnmolche. – Reptilia Nr. 67 12 (5): 16 – 35.

Blanck, T., Braun, M. (2007): Zur Haltung und Zucht des gebänderten Tigersalamanders – *Ambystoma mavortium*. – Reptilia Nr.67 12 (5): 36 – 40.

Benthien, J. (2014): Haltung und Nachzucht der Tigersalamander. – Terraria Nr. 49: 14 – 23

Pasmans, F., Bogaerts, S., Janssen, H., Sparreboom, M. (2014): Molche & Salamander – NTV Verlag, 247 S.

Wawrzyniak, H.,(1994): Zur Umwandlungsproblematik des Axolotls – Das Aquarium Nr. 304: 21 – 24

GLOSSARY

Albinism:	The inability to synthesize the color pigment melanin (black)
Ampullar organ:	An organ for detecting electrical fields, e.g., those emitted by other organisms
Aquatic:	Living in water
Class:	A high taxonomic unit, grouping, e.g., all amphibians (tailed and tailless) in the class Amphibia
Chromosome:	The entirety of genetic information stored in a body cell
Crowding effect:	Ecological measure for self-controlling the number of individuals at a level where the available resources can sustain the population inhabiting a habitat
Estivation:	A period of summery dormancy (also spelled aestivation)
Ethology:	The science of behavior and behavioral expressions
Facultative (neoteny):	Possible, but not necessarily required; amphibians may metamorphose or remain at larval stage
Family:	A taxonomic unit, grouping, e.g., all Mole Salamanders in the family *Ambystoma*tidae
Gene pool:	The entirety of the genetic variability in the individuals of a population

Genetic manifestation:	The anchoring of a trait in the genetic composition
Genus:	A taxonomic unit, grouping more closely related species together, e.g., all True Mole Salamanders in the genus *Ambystoma* (italicized); pl. genera
Gynogenesis:	Development of egg cells upon penetration of sperm cells, but without the use of the male chromosomes
Heterosis effect:	An effect from the cross-breeding of two species that will produce offspring that are more vital and fertile than either of the parent species
Hibernation:	A period of wintery dormancy
Hybridizing:	The cross-breeding of different taxa (genera, species, subspecies, bloodlines)
Hyoid pump:	A mechanism for acquiring prey through creating negative pressure by the rapid depression of the hyoid bone while opening the mouth
Hypomelanism:	The reduced presence of dark pigment in the skin
Inducible obligatory neoteny:	A form of neoteny that can be overcome by inducing metamorphosis under experimental circumstances
Cladistic:	Systematic relationships as derived from the reconstructed evolutionary lines of taxa

Cloaca:	The joint exit opening for feces and sexual products (sperm, eggs)
Cloacal glands:	A set of skin-embedded glands in the re gion of the cloaca
Lateral line organ:	A sensory organ for detecting changes in pressure on the head and flanks of fish and aquatic amphibians or their larvae
Melanism:	An abnormal increase in the amount of black pigment in the skin, a.k.a. Hypermelanism
Metamorphosis:	In amphibians, the transformation from an aquatic larval form into a terrestrial animal by means of restructuring physical structures
Mitochondrial:	Referring to structures in certain cell organelles (mitochondriae)
Morphology:	The science of the structure and shape of organisms and their body parts
Mutation:	The spontaneous or intended (through selective breeding) change of the genetic composition
Neoteny:	Reaching sexual maturity at larval stage
Neozoans:	Deliberately or accidentally introduced, non-native species
Obligatory (neoteny):	Bound to a certain condition; larval amphibians *will never* metamorphose, not even when exposed to the respective hormones

Order:	A high taxonomic unit, grouping, e.g., all tailed amphibians in the order Caudata
Oviposition:	The deposition of eggs
Pathogen:	A "germ" that will cause disease
Pheromone:	A volatile substance that carries information from one individual of a species to another
Phenotype:	The appearance of an individual as determined by its genetic composition (genotype)
Pineal organ:	An evolutionary very old, photosensitive organ situated in the forehead
Population:	A colony of individuals of the same taxon that inhabits a certain geographic region
Receptor:	Sensory cells that will detect certain cues
Recessive:	Suppressed genetic information that will not affect the phenotype
Rehydration:	The replenishment of deficient body fluids through the intake of water
Secondary sexual traits:	Sex-indicative differences in the appearance of representatives of the same taxon
Species:	The basic taxonomic unit, grouping closely related individuals together, e.g., all Tiger Salamanders as the species *Ambystoma tigrinum* (italicized)
Spermatophore:	A "packet" of sperm, consisting of a jelly portion and a clump of sperm cells

Subspecies:	A taxonomic subunit within a species, grouping populations of a species that can be identified as being more closely related among each other than to other populations of the same species, e.g.. *Ambystoma mavortium nebulosum* (italicized)
Symbiosis:	Meaning "living together", the often intricate cooperative co-existence of two or more life forms to the benefit of all
Systematics:	A discipline of biology that assesses the diversity of organisms and arranges the groups obtained thus in a hierarchic system
Tactile:	Referring to the sense of touch
Taxon:	A systematic unit, e.g., species, subspecies, genus, family, etc. (pl. taxa)
Taxonomy:	A subdiscipline of systematics that describes groups of life forms (taxa), provides them with scientific names, delimits them from others, and arranges them in a systematic system according to their degree of relatedness
Territorial:	A behavioral disposition that serves maintaining a pool of essential resources (the territory) for the exclusive use by an individual
Torsion:	The twisting of a structure along its long axis
Triploid:	Triplicated sets of chromosomes in the body cells of an organism